SECRETS TO STEWARDING GOD'S VOICE IN A NEW ERA WORKBOOK

THE POWER AND PRICE OF INFLUENCE

JEREMIAH JOHNSON

DESTINY IMAGE

CONTENTS

INTRODUCTION

INTRODUCTION TO *SECRETS TO STEWARDING GOD'S VOICE IN A NEW ERA OFFICIAL WORKBOOK*

Welcome to a transformative journey that invites you into a deeper understanding and stewardship of God's voice in our lives. As you engage with this workbook, you are stepping into a curated series of teachings and reflections designed to equip and inspire you to recognize and respond to God's call with wisdom and courage in this new era.

Throughout this workbook, you will explore key themes that are both timeless and particularly pertinent to our current spiritual landscape. From understanding the prophetic gifts and God's guidance in our decisions, to walking in the fear of the Lord and recognizing the power of the Holy Spirit in our daily lives, each chapter builds upon the next, crafting a comprehensive pathway toward deeper spiritual maturity.

KEY TAKEAWAYS FROM THIS WORKBOOK:

- **Deepening Your Understanding of God's Voice:** You will explore what it means to truly hear God, distinguishing His voice from the noise of the world and our own desires. This journey will challenge you to refine your spiritual senses through scriptural insights and practical guidance.
- **Embracing the Fear of the Lord:** In an age where the concept of fearing God is often misunderstood, you will rediscover the beauty and necessity of this biblical mandate. This fear is not about timidity but about living in awe and reverence of God's holiness, which in turn shapes our character and decisions.
- **Stewardship of Prophetic Gifts:** As you delve into the dynamics of prophecy and the role of prophets in the church today, you will learn how to responsibly handle the weighty yet empowering gift of prophecy. This includes how to share prophetic insights in a way that edifies the church and aligns with God's will.
- **Navigating the Challenges of Influence:** This workbook will address the temptations and pitfalls that come with spiritual and social influence, teaching you how to remain humble and rooted in Christ amidst success and visibility.
- **Engaging in Spiritual Warfare:** Understanding and engaging in spiritual warfare is crucial for stewarding God's voice. You will gain insights into the armor of God and how to use it effectively to protect yourself and advance God's Kingdom.

- **The Role of Prayer and Intercession:** Learn the significance of prayer as a foundational practice for engaging with God's voice. Through dedicated prayer and intercession, you will see how God's plans and purposes are revealed and brought to fruition.
- **Building Godly Relationships:** Discover the importance of cultivating relationships that align with divine purposes, focusing on partnerships that foster spiritual growth and kingdom advancement.
- **Application of Scriptural Wisdom:** Each chapter is deeply rooted in Scripture, offering you a solid theological framework to apply God's Word in practical, life-changing ways.
- **Transformation through Trials:** Learn how God uses trials and challenges not only to speak to us but also to transform us, preparing us for the roles He has designed for us within His grand narrative.
- **Living Out Your Divine Calling:** Ultimately, this workbook aims to equip you to live out your divine calling with confidence and clarity, ensuring that your life's.

CHAPTER 1

THE SECRET TO INFLUENCE AND LEGACY

Remember, true greatness in the kingdom of God is not measured by how many follow you, but by how faithfully you follow Christ and lead others to do the same. Let humility and integrity be the hallmarks of your influence.

"But he who is greatest among you shall be your servant." - Matthew 23:11 (NKJV)

As we embark on this exploration of influence and legacy, I've come to see through my own experiences how both challenging and rewarding this path can be. It's not just about having a position of power; it's about how you manage that power and the responsibilities that come with it.

Influence Requires Stewardship. This insight hit me later in life. Initially, I saw influence merely as a means to lead and make big decisions. However, I learned that it's really about nurturing and carefully managing the trust you're given.

The Cost of Influence can be steep. With the visible successes come hidden struggles: losing friends, enduring public criticism, and keeping your inner self aligned with your outward actions. I've felt the weight of these costs deeply, and they've taught me the importance of resilience.

Growing up, I was quite naïve about what it would take to fulfill the prophetic words spoken over my life. This naivety led me to underestimate the difficulties ahead. **Early Naivety Can Lead to Challenges** in realizing how tough the journey can be.

The Bible and church history show us that many leaders, even those who began their journeys with promise, often faltered. Leaders like King Uzziah and Saul started well but eventually lost their way due to pride and disobedience. These stories serve as warnings and are crucial as **Biblical Examples of Leadership Pitfalls**.

One thing has become increasingly clear to me over the years: **The Importance of Private Integrity for Public Influence**. The downfall of many leaders, both in scripture and in more recent times, often stems from a lack of integrity away from the public eye.

Attacks and Testing Come with Influence. This is a hard truth. As your influence grows, so does the target on your back. You will face jealousy, misunderstandings, and even spiritual attacks. Learning to differentiate between God's testing and malicious attacks has been key to my perseverance.

In today's digital world, **The Allure of Self-Promotion** is stronger than ever. It's easy to get caught up in how you're perceived online. But I've learned that genuine influence isn't measured by likes or shares but by the real impact you have on others.

A major lesson I've learned is that **Stewarding Influence Means Pointing to Christ**. It's not about me. My purpose is to direct people to Him, to be a vessel for His truth and love.

Influence as a Tool for Kingdom Purposes has reshaped my understanding of my role. Influence isn't just about personal success; it's a tool God provides to serve His kingdom, like Esther or Samuel, who were placed by God in positions to enact His divine plans.

Lastly, the real **Legacy of Influence** isn't about how you are remembered but about the impact you make on others. It's about planting seeds of faith, hope, and love that will grow long after you're gone.

REFLECTIVE QUESTIONS

1. What personal sacrifices have you experienced or anticipate facing in your pursuit of influence?
2. How do you ensure that your private life upholds the same standards of integrity that you display publicly?
3. In what ways can you better prepare to handle the criticisms and attacks that may come with increased influence?
4. How can you guard against the temptations of pride and self-promotion in your leadership role?
5. What steps can you take to use your influence more effectively for God's kingdom purposes?

ACTIONABLE STEPS

- **Cultivate a Life of Humility**: Regularly assess your motives and actions to ensure they align with Christ's example of servitude. This may involve seeking accountability from trusted spiritual leaders or mentors.

- **Equip Yourself with Biblical Wisdom**: Engage deeply with the Scriptures to understand the principles of godly leadership and influence. Study the lives of biblical figures who managed their influence well and those who did not.
- **Engage in Prayer and Fasting**: Dedicate time to seek God's guidance on how to handle influence. Prayer and fasting can sharpen your spiritual discernment, helping you navigate the complexities of leadership.

JOURNALING **Prompt**

Reflect on a recent situation where you had to exercise influence. Did you feel you managed it with integrity and humility? What could you have done differently, and what did you learn from this experience that could help you grow in your ability to steward influence wisely?

CHAPTER 2

DON'T DESPISE YOUR YOUTH

Remember, true greatness in the kingdom of God is not measured by how many follow you, but by how faithfully you follow Christ and lead others to do the same. Let humility and integrity be the hallmarks of your influence.

"But he who is greatest among you shall be your servant." - Matthew 23:11 (NKJV)

From the time I was 12, I knew God was calling me to preach. My father, a pastor himself, encouraged me to start right away, suggesting I reach out to the needy. This led me to spend many years serving at a local mission, sharing God's word with those less fortunate. These early experiences, far from the limelight and without any digital applause, were crucial in shaping my ministry's foundation.

Throughout my teenage years, I continued to preach wherever possible, from detention centers for young people to retirement homes, and even on mission trips. I learned to deliver sermons in places without microphones, social media, or any form of recognition. This taught me that **true ministry isn't about the size of your audience but your commitment to God's call.**

The road to genuine influence often starts with unnoticed, humble acts of service. Today, I see many young people dreaming of big stages and wide influence. However, when I suggest they start small—by ministering to the poor or serving in less glamorous settings—they sometimes feel slighted. This reaction shows a troubling **sense of entitlement** and a misunderstanding of what true ministry involves.

Through years of faithfully serving in small, challenging places, God prepared me for larger opportunities. Now, I speak to large audiences around the nation and the world. But remembering where I started and the lessons I learned is crucial.

Each step of my journey, including the early days at the mission and preaching to unresponsive or challenging audiences, was vital. They taught me that **Influence Should Not Be Sought For Personal Gain** but as a means to serve others more effectively. Whether I was addressing a few sleepy seniors or a group of resistant youth, each moment was an opportunity to grow in faithfulness and perseverance.

As my ministry expanded, so did the opportunities, but also the challenges and temptations. **The allure of fame and success** can be enticing. However, the pressures and expectations that come with public recognition can distort one's priorities if not deeply rooted in a personal commitment to Christ.

The desire for recognition and the risks of entitlement can corrupt the pure motives of ministry. It's essential to maintain **humility and purity of heart**, which I continually strive to do. I remind myself and others that the greatest leaders in God's kingdom are not those with the largest platforms but those who serve with the most humility and devotion.

Navigating the world of ministry and influence requires a

steadfast commitment to serving others, regardless of the platform size or the recognition it may bring. It's about staying true to God's call, serving faithfully, and ensuring that our actions always align with His will.

As we continue on this path, let us always remember to keep our motives pure, our hearts humble, and our service genuine. **True greatness in God's kingdom isn't measured by how many people follow us but by how faithfully we follow Christ** and lead others to do the same.

REFLECTIVE QUESTIONS

1. What personal sacrifices have you experienced or anticipate facing in your pursuit of influence?
2. How do you ensure that your private life upholds the same standards of integrity that you display publicly?
3. In what ways can you better prepare to handle the criticisms and attacks that may come with increased influence?
4. How can you guard against the temptations of pride and self-promotion in your leadership role?
5. What steps can you take to use your influence more effectively for God's kingdom purposes?

ACTIONABLE STEPS

- **Cultivate a Life of Humility**: Regularly assess your motives and actions to ensure they align with Christ's example of servitude. This may involve seeking accountability from trusted spiritual leaders or mentors.

- **Equip Yourself with Biblical Wisdom**: Engage deeply with the Scriptures to understand the principles of godly leadership and influence. Study the lives of biblical figures who managed their influence well and those who did not.
- **Engage in Prayer and Fasting**: Dedicate time to seek God's guidance on how to handle influence. Prayer and fasting can sharpen your spiritual discernment, helping you navigate the complexities of leadership.

JOURNALING **Prompt**

Reflect on a recent situation where you had to exercise influence. Did you feel you managed it with integrity and humility? What could you have done differently, and what did you learn from this experience that could help you grow in your ability to steward influence wisely?

CHAPTER 3

THE DANGERS OF CELEBRITY CHRISTIANITY

Remember, true greatness in the kingdom of God is not measured by how many follow you, but by how faithfully you follow Christ and lead others to do the same. Let humility and integrity be the hallmarks of your influence.

"But he who is greatest among you shall be your servant." - Matthew 23:11 (NKJV)

In this chapter, I delve into a critical issue facing the Christian community today: the influence of what I call "Celebrity Christianity." We are at a pivotal moment where God is clearly distinguishing who genuinely follows His teachings on crucial issues like abortion, sexual immorality, and honesty.

This era might seem daunting, but it is actually **a blessing**. It's crucial to understand that while division in the Church often carries negative connotations—mostly due to misuse like slander or deceit—the type of division I'm talking about here is both healthy and necessary. It's about making clear distinctions between those who uphold God's Word and those who don't.

Paul talked about this in 1 Corinthians when he mentioned that **divisions must occur to highlight those who genuinely follow Christ.** This isn't about causing conflict for the sake of conflict; it's about purifying the Church to achieve genuine unity. This process might sound harsh, but it's meant to separate the true teachings of the gospel from harmful distortions that creep into church doctrines.

As we witness these changes, it's normal to feel a mix of grief and betrayal, especially when leaders or institutions we trust are called out for not adhering to biblical principles. This shake-up isn't just a random occurrence; it's a **divine intervention** meant to bring clarity and purification to the Church.

During my time in ministry, I've faced numerous pressures to conform to a more palatable version of Christianity. Influential figures have often suggested that I avoid speaking on divisive issues like holiness or repentance to maintain and grow my audience. Despite these pressures, I've chosen to stick firmly to the messages God has called me to deliver, regardless of the personal or professional cost.

This stance has not been without its challenges. I've often found myself at odds with mainstream Christian culture, which sometimes favors a more diluted gospel that appeals to a broader audience. The temptation to soften the gospel's harder truths can be overwhelming, especially when doing so might lead to greater fame or financial gain.

Yet, each time I'm faced with the choice to compromise, I am reminded of why I began my ministry. It was never about gaining fame or wealth—it was about **spreading the truth of God's Word.** Staying true to this mission has sometimes led to isolation and criticism, but it has also deepened my commitment to preaching the gospel as it is, **not as others wish it to be.**

Navigating through this celebrity-driven Christian landscape requires vigilance and a **strong commitment to biblical truths**. We must be wary of the lure of popularity and the potential to water down our messages for broader acceptance. Our primary allegiance is to God and His Word, not to the fleeting approval of the public.

As we go forward, let us embrace the necessary **divisions** that help clarify who we are and what we stand for in the faith. Let's view these challenging times as opportunities to strengthen our testimony and commitment to Christ, knowing that our faithfulness will lead to a purer, more robust Christian witness in the world.

Whether speaking to a few or to thousands, whether compensated richly or not at all, remember to **stay true to the call God has placed on your life**. The true measure of our ministry isn't found in the size of our platforms or the number of our followers but in our fidelity to the gospel and our effectiveness in leading others closer to Christ.

REFLECTIVE QUESTIONS

1. What personal sacrifices have you experienced or anticipate facing in your pursuit of influence?
2. How do you ensure that your private life upholds the same standards of integrity that you display publicly?
3. In what ways can you better prepare to handle the criticisms and attacks that may come with increased influence?
4. How can you guard against the temptations of pride and self-promotion in your leadership role?
5. What steps can you take to use your influence more effectively for God's kingdom purposes?

. . .

ACTIONABLE STEPS

- **Cultivate a Life of Humility**: Regularly assess your motives and actions to ensure they align with Christ's example of servitude. This may involve seeking accountability from trusted spiritual leaders or mentors.
- **Equip Yourself with Biblical Wisdom**: Engage deeply with the Scriptures to understand the principles of godly leadership and influence. Study the lives of biblical figures who managed their influence well and those who did not.
- **Engage in Prayer and Fasting**: Dedicate time to seek God's guidance on how to handle influence. Prayer and fasting can sharpen your spiritual discernment, helping you navigate the complexities of leadership.

JOURNALING Prompt

Reflect on a recent situation where you had to exercise influence. Did you feel you managed it with integrity and humility? What could you have done differently, and what did you learn from this experience that could help you grow in your ability to steward influence wisely?

CHAPTER 4

HEALTHY COMMUNITY AND ACCOUNTABILITY

Embrace the support of a healthy community and strong accountability; these are essential for success and stability in all areas of life.

"But as for me and my house, we will serve the Lord." - Joshua 24:15 (NKJV)

Having influence is a profound responsibility that brings with it the potential for significant impact, both positive and negative. The journey is fraught with opportunities for success as well as risks of failure. **Long-term success**, however, isn't just about having influence; it fundamentally hinges on the presence of a **healthy community and robust accountability**. These elements are crucial because they help you navigate the complexities of influence with integrity and wisdom.

Throughout my journey, I've realized how vital a supportive community and strong accountability mechanisms are to maintaining a balanced and healthy personal and professional life. I

19

can't overstate the importance of being surrounded by people who **genuinely love and care for you** for who you are—not just what you can offer them or their hidden agendas to benefit from your status.

My life, marriage, and family have profoundly benefited from being part of a **vibrant local church**. This community has not only provided a space for growth and healing but has also been a bedrock of support through various challenges. It's in this setting that spiritual parents and mentors have played a critical role, helping us navigate both the blessings of growing influence and the inevitable spiritual battles that come with it.

However, the path hasn't always been smooth. We've had to establish strong boundaries to protect ourselves from individuals who, despite initial appearances, turned out to have intentions of causing harm rather than offering **genuine friendship**. Learning to discern these motives has been an essential skill developed over time.

The local church has been **instrumental in keeping me grounded.** While traveling and speaking engagements provide a certain level of external validation, it's the day-to-day interactions and relationships within my local church that truly test and reveal the authenticity of my faith and leadership. These are the people who see beyond the public persona to the real person behind the scenes—they witness how I interact with my family, handle stress, and live out my faith in everyday situations.

This chapter explores the critical difference between having a **temporary impact** through public speaking and cultivating **lasting fruit** through deep, consistent community involvement. It's easy to impress from a distance, but true spiritual fruit comes from close, genuine relationships and ongoing personal development.

One major risk for influencers, particularly in the age of social media, is the temptation to substitute online interactions for deep, **face-to-face relationships**. Many influencers manage to create an idealized image online, but lack a local, accountable community that truly knows them. This disconnect can lead to a superficial faith that crumbles under pressure.

In today's Christian community, there's a concerning trend where success is often measured by worldly standards such as popularity and financial success, rather than **obedience to God's will.** This misalignment can lead individuals away from the foundational principles of faith, causing them to prioritize personal gain over spiritual integrity.

Tragically, the Christian community has witnessed numerous leaders who began their ministries with pure intentions but fell into moral compromise due to a lack of accountability. These falls from grace often start with a gradual withdrawal from community life and accountability, leading to isolation where sin can fester unchecked.

Several years ago, Dutch Sheets—a respected leader—publicly addressed this issue. He admitted that our community often lacks discernment, elevating individuals based on charisma or talent rather than character and maturity. This has led to inappropriate people being placed in positions of influence, sometimes even affecting national leadership.

This reflection brings me back to a personal turning point in my life, a profound conversation with Dutch Sheets at a conference. This dialogue highlighted the essential tests every young influencer faces: character, intellect, and wisdom. Dutch pointed out my need for greater wisdom to balance the significant revelations and visions I had received. His advice was a stark reminder of the **weight of responsibility that comes with influence.**

This chapter underscores the **importance of humility,** the need for genuine community ties, and the wisdom that comes from living in close fellowship with others who can provide **honest feedback and guidance.** No matter the size of the audience or platform, the core principles of integrity, humility, and accountability remain the same. These principles ensure that as our influence grows, so does our commitment to live out our faith authentically and impactfully.

REFLECTIVE QUESTIONS

1. How do you identify individuals who genuinely support you versus those with self-serving motives?
2. What role has your local church played in your personal and spiritual development?
3. Can you recall a time when community support helped you overcome a challenge?
4. How do you maintain accountability in your relationships?
5. What steps can you take to strengthen your community ties and accountability mechanisms?

ACTIONABLE STEPS

- **Cultivate Authentic Relationships**: Invest time in building genuine relationships within your local church. Seek out individuals who encourage spiritual growth and offer honest feedback.
- **Equip Yourself with Mentors**: Identify and approach potential mentors who exemplify spiritual maturity and integrity. Regular mentorship can provide guidance and prevent missteps.
- **Engage in Transparent Communication**: Foster openness and honesty in your interactions to ensure

that your relationships are built on trust and mutual respect.

23

JOURNALING **Prompt**

Reflect on your current circle of influence. Are there people within this circle who challenge you to grow and hold you accountable? How can you engage more deeply with these individuals to foster a healthier community?

CHAPTER 5

OVERCOMING JEALOUSY

Let's stand firm in the truth that God is greater than our hearts and He knows everything. There is no need to fear the jealousy of others when we are secure in His love.

"For if our heart condemns us, God is greater than our heart, and knows all things." 1 John 3:20 -

Anyone who has ever accomplished something significant for God has likely faced the sting of jealousy from others, even from people they've never met. It's a tough truth: jealousy is not just any sin—it's a gateway to all kinds of harmful actions **(James 3:16)**. That's both shocking and a stark reminder for us to stay vigilant.

Paul's words to the Corinthians are clear: jealousy and strife show that someone is living by the flesh, not the spirit **(1 Corinthians 3:3)**. And in Galatians, jealousy is listed as a work of the flesh **(Galatians 5:19-21)**. It directly threatens our spiritual well-being and the unity of our communities.

R.T. Kendall describes jealousy as resentment over someone

else's success, which can lead to actions aimed at damaging the successful person's reputation. This toxic behavior can destroy relationships and create divisions within communities, as people act out of spite rather than support.

At its core, jealousy stems from a feeling of anger and resentment that someone else has something we lack. It's a deeply evil and manipulative emotion that can even drive people to extreme actions, like when Cain killed Abel out of envy (**1 John 3:12**), or Joseph's brothers sold him into slavery, unable to bear the special love their father had for him (**Genesis 37:11**).

Growing in influence invariably attracts jealousy. This is a harsh reality of leadership and success. Some think that by walking in humility, they can avoid envy, but even Jesus, who embodied humility, was arrested and crucified out of jealousy (**Mark 15:10**).

Accepting that jealousy is part of leadership is essential for anyone called to lead. It's vital to understand that not everyone will celebrate your achievements; some might even resent them. While this doesn't mean accepting poor treatment, it does mean we should be prepared for it and learn to **handle it gracefully**.

Leaders must face the tough reality that their actions and intentions will often be misunderstood by those who view them through a lens of jealousy. This is especially challenging for pioneers who, by nature, **disrupt the status quo** and can become easy targets for criticism and false accusations.

In my book *Prophetic Pioneering*, I address how pioneers can't fulfill God's will without challenging established norms and causing significant changes in the body of Christ. This inevitably leads to many stumbling, scoffing, and criticizing, often fueled by a spirit of jealousy. The source of many such attacks is people's own desires to possess what those with influence have.

Handling these challenges requires more than resilience; it demands **spiritual maturity.** Leaders must learn not to base their peace on people's approval but on their relationship with God. Often, the very criticisms meant to destroy them can instead refine and strengthen their character if they **respond with humility and faith**.

The stark reality is that both God and the enemy want a pioneer to "die" in a sense—Satan seeks their destruction; God aims for their refinement. The true peace and fulfillment you seek as a leader come from dying to the need for human approval and **living for God's approval alone.**

Navigating leadership and influence involves continually facing and overcoming the spirit of jealousy. It's about maintaining your integrity and focus amid misunderstanding and hostility. Remember, the greater the calling, the greater the opposition, but also the greater the potential for profound spiritual growth and effectiveness in your mission.

REFLECTIVE QUESTIONS

1. Have you ever experienced jealousy from others due to your achievements or influence? How did it make you feel?
2. Why do you think people become jealous even of those they do not know personally?
3. How can we guard our hearts against harboring jealousy towards others who succeed?
4. What role does humility play in combating jealousy?
5. Can you identify a situation where you felt misunderstood due to the jealousy of others? How did you handle it?

ACTIONABLE STEPS

- **Cultivate** a culture of celebration in your interactions with others to counteract the roots of jealousy.
- **Equip** yourself with the knowledge of God's word concerning jealousy and how it can destroy communities.
- **Engage** in transparent conversations with mentors or spiritual leaders about your struggles with jealousy, seeking wisdom and guidance.

JOURNALING Prompt

Reflect on a time when you felt the impact of jealousy, either from within yourself or from others. How did it affect your actions and relationships? What steps can you take to ensure you handle such feelings constructively in the future?

CHAPTER 6

THE WAR BETWEEN SAUL AND DAVID

Let your heart be steadfast, always set on seeking the Lord. No matter the trials or the tribulations, remember, He is your rock and your redeemer.

Psalm 105:4 - Seek the Lord and His strength; Seek His face evermore!

In my exploration of the lives of King Saul and David, I discovered two distinct leadership styles shaped by their hearts. While Saul was overwhelmed by **jealousy** and fear of losing his throne, David, despite his own faults, had a heart tuned to God's will. Saul's leadership demonstrates the peril of being controlled by **insecurity** and the need to maintain power. His inability to nurture true spiritual growth and empower others like David starkly contrasts with David's approach when he later became king.

The critical part of Saul's story for me was his reluctance to genuinely empower David. He viewed David as a **rival** rather than a successor. This approach is a cautionary tale about the effects of fear-driven leadership, as it hindered spiritual and leadership development within his kingdom. On the other hand, David's story, particularly his time in Engedi, taught him to **depend on God** rather than on human approval or worldly success.

David's refusal to harm Saul, even when opportunities presented themselves, highlights his respect for God's anointed and his understanding of **divine timing**. His **patience and humility** in waiting for God's timing rather than seizing power prematurely are lessons that resonate deeply with anyone in a leadership role.

This chapter not only looks at their external conflicts but also at their internal spiritual struggles. It offers profound insights into how the **condition of our heart** affects our leadership and underscores the importance of aligning our ambitions with God's directives.

REFLECTIVE QUESTIONS

1. What personal insecurities can lead you to view others as competitors rather than collaborators?
2. How can the story of David and Saul help you reflect on the importance of waiting for God's timing in your own life?
3. In what ways can fear of losing control manifest in your personal or professional relationships?
4. How does the idea of 'divine timing' change your approach to leadership and influence?
5. Can you identify a situation where you need to show more patience or humility?

ACTIONABLE STEPS

Cultivate: Develop a deeper sense of humility by regularly reflecting on the story of David at Engedi, considering how you can apply his patience and reliance on God in your own leadership roles.

Equip: Arm yourself with the knowledge of Scripture related to leadership and God's timing, such as the stories of Saul and David, to better discern when to act and when to yield.

Engage: Engage in open dialogue with mentors or spiritual leaders about how to handle jealousy and competition, seeking their wisdom and integrating their insights into your personal growth strategy.

JOURNALING Prompt

Reflect on a time when you felt threatened by someone else's success. How did you react, and what could you have done differently to align your response more closely with David's example of humility and trust in God's plan?

～

CHAPTER 7

THE DECEITFULNESS OF SIN

Stand strong in your faith and let no temptation sway you from the path of righteousness.

"No temptation has overtaken you except such as is common to man; but God is faithful, who will not allow you to be tempted beyond what you are able, but with the temptation will also make the way of escape, that you may be able to bear it." (1 Corinthians 10:13 NKJV)

I n this chapter, let's dive deep into the deceptive nature of sin and the incredible power of redemption offered through **Jesus Christ**. Sin has a tricky way of making us believe we're gaining something beneficial when, in reality, it robs us of the true joys and deep connections we seek in life. This deception begins from the very first sin in the Garden of Eden, where the serpent convinced Eve to eat from the forbidden tree. This act promised knowledge and pleasure but **delivered separation from God**—a gap that Isaiah the prophet described as a consequence of our **iniquities separating** us from God.

When sin entered, fear and shame were close behind. Adam and Eve, who had once walked freely with God, suddenly found themselves hiding out of **fear**, realizing their nakedness and feeling profound shame. **Before sin,** there was no fear, no shame, no hiding from God. Their choice to sin changed their relationship with God, introducing fear of His presence, which was a new and terrifying feeling for them.

Additionally, sin distorted their ability to accept responsibility. Faced with God's questions, Adam quickly blamed Eve and even God Himself, suggesting that the fault lay with the companion God had provided him. This shift from personal responsibility to blame is a direct result of sin **corrupting human nature.**

This narrative is crucial because it showcases the profound effects of sin—fear, shame, and blame—and the powerful deceit at its core. Sin sells itself as a path to greater joy, but it leads to loss and separation from true happiness found **only in God's presence.**

Yet, the story doesn't end in despair, thanks to **Jesus Christ**. Where Adam and Eve failed, Jesus succeeded. In the Garden of Gethsemane, He chose **submission to God's will** over His own desires, effectively reversing the curse of Eden. His sacrifice on the Cross and His **victory over death** not only paid the penalty for our sins but also provided a way for us to live free from sin's grip.

For us today, especially those in positions of influence, embracing this truth is vital. We are called to lead by example, living out the freedom Christ won for us, showing the world what it means to **walk in His grace**, free from the deception and destruction of sin.

This chapter aims to guide us in understanding and applying these truths. As we grasp the depth of sin's deception and the transformative power of Christ's redemption, our daily lives should **reflect** this understanding, influencing how we handle temptations, relate to others, and make decisions. Our challenge is to consistently choose the path of righteousness, illuminated by Christ's teachings, enabling us to lead lives that truly glorify God.

REFLECTIVE QUESTIONS

1. How have you experienced the deceitfulness of sin in your own life?
2. In what ways can you identify with Adam and Eve's reaction to sin in terms of fear and shame?
3. How does understanding Jesus' victory over sin change your approach to dealing with temptation?
4. What steps can you take to ensure you are leading others away from sin and towards righteousness?
5. How can the church better equip its members to recognize and resist the subtleties of sin?

ACTIONABLE STEPS

- **Cultivate** a daily practice of reflecting on the nature of Jesus' sacrifice to deepen your gratitude and commitment to living righteously.
- **Equip** yourself and others with biblical truths about sin and redemption by organizing or attending Bible study sessions focused on these themes.
- **Engage** with a community of believers to hold each other accountable, providing support and encouragement to live out the truth of the Gospel.

. . .

JOURNALING Prompt

Reflect on a recent challenge where you felt tempted or misled. Write about how you responded versus how you might respond differently in the future, using the principles learned in this chapter about the deceitfulness of sin and the power of Christ's redemption.

∽

CHAPTER 8

UPROOTING THE SPIRIT OF REJECTION

You are not defined by the rejection you face. You are defined by God's acceptance.

"He is despised and rejected by men, A Man of sorrows and acquainted with grief. And we hid, as it were, our faces from Him; He was despised, and we did not esteem Him." Isaiah 53:3 NKJV

In this chapter, I delve into the unavoidable reality of rejection that accompanies anyone who steps into a role of influence, using Daniel as a prime example. Despite his exceptional qualities and the favor he found in King Darius's eyes, **Daniel was not immune** to jealousy or false accusations from his contemporaries. This dual experience of acceptance and rejection is a common thread for those following their **God-given paths**.

Throughout Scripture, we see that the most devoted followers of God often faced intense rejection. From Moses, who endured constant complaints from the Israelites, to Jesus Christ

—who faced the ultimate rejection—these stories underscore that **rejection is an expected**, though challenging, part of spiritual leadership.

However, it is critical to distinguish between typical rejection and harboring a spirit of rejection. The latter can lead to a bitter, victim-like perspective that taints one's interactions with the world. It's vital to ask ourselves: Are we just dealing with rejection, or are we viewing our lives through the lens of a **spirit of rejection**?

This chapter emphasizes the importance of overcoming the spirit of rejection by following the example set by Jesus Christ. Despite widespread rejection, Jesus never let a spirit of rejection take root within Him because He understood that **His acceptance came from God**, not from the people around Him.

By embracing our identity in God's acceptance, we can confront and overcome the spirit of rejection. This allows us to face opposition with resilience and maintain a healthy perspective, free from the bitterness and suspicion that can so easily cloud our judgment.

Ultimately, this chapter calls us to examine and uproot any spirit of rejection we might carry, enabling us to pursue our divine destinies with clarity and confidence, irrespective of the challenges we might face.

REFLECTIVE QUESTIONS

1. How can you tell if you're dealing with just rejection or a spirit of rejection in your life?
2. What steps can you take to prevent a spirit of rejection from taking root in your response to everyday opposition?

3. How has understanding your identity in Christ changed how you handle rejection?

4. What similarities do you find between your experiences of rejection and those faced by biblical figures like Daniel or Moses?

5. How does realizing that Jesus also faced rejection impact your feelings towards your own experiences of rejection?

ACTIONABLE STEPS

- **Cultivate** a deep understanding of your identity in Christ by daily meditating on Scriptures that affirm God's love and acceptance.
- **Equip** yourself with tools to handle rejection constructively by seeking mentorship or counseling that focuses on spiritual and emotional health.
- **Engage** in community with others who uplift and support you, allowing you to share your burdens and find encouragement in your walk of faith.

JOURNALING Prompt

Reflect on a recent experience of rejection. Write about how it made you feel, and then contrast those feelings with the truth of what God says about you. How can this understanding help you the next time you face rejection?

CHAPTER 9
NAVIGATING SPIRITUAL WARFARE

Stay grounded in your faith, knowing that your challenges extend beyond earthly issues; they are battles fought in the spiritual realms with divine support.

"For we do not wrestle against flesh and blood, but against principalities, against powers, against the rulers of the darkness of this age, against spiritual hosts of wickedness in the heavenly places." Ephesians 6:12 NKJV

In this chapter, I delve into spiritual warfare, an inevitable challenge for anyone with significant influence. The Bible clarifies in Ephesians 6:12 that our true conflict is with spiritual forces, not merely the immediate problems or opposition we face. This type of warfare tends to intensify during pivotal moments such as when initiating new endeavors or undergoing significant changes.

Consider the story of Moses. At his birth, Pharaoh issued a decree to kill all Hebrew firstborns to eliminate any potential threats to his reign. However, Moses survived through **divine intervention**. A similar scenario unfolded during the birth of Jesus when King Herod ordered the massacre of Bethlehem's infant boys in his attempt to kill Jesus, which also failed because of a **protective dream** given to Joseph.

These historical examples underscore a consistent pattern: Whenever God is about to initiate something significant, Satan intervenes with attempts to destroy it. The timing of such attacks is often during:

1. **Seasons of birthing**—when new ventures or movements are being started.
2. **Seasons of transition**—when significant changes are taking place.

Even Jesus experienced this. Before embarking on His ministry, He was tempted by Satan during a vulnerable moment following a 40-day fast in the wilderness. Though tempted, Jesus resisted, showcasing His **spiritual fortitude**.

Furthermore, various roles within the church are susceptible to specific types of spiritual attacks:

- **Apostles** often face assaults from the Leviathan spirit, a force that breeds division, particularly when establishing new churches.
- **Prophets** may encounter the Jezebel spirit, which aims to silence and control them.
- **Teachers** can be targeted by a religious spirit, which seeks to suffocate the life-giving nature of Scripture through legalism.
- **Pastors** are prone to attacks of discouragement, which can sap their joy and lead to despair.
- **Evangelists** might struggle with vanity, which shifts

their focus from their mission to personal fame and recognition.

Awareness of these targeted attacks and their timing is crucial for maintaining vigilance and readiness to counteract them. Recognizing that Satan constantly seeks to thwart God's plans is essential for preparing ourselves to withstand these challenges.

REFLECTIVE QUESTIONS

1. How do you identify spiritual warfare in your life, and what steps do you take to address it?
2. What similarities do you see between your experiences and the biblical examples mentioned?
3. In what ways can you prepare for spiritual attacks during key life transitions?
4. How can church leaders support one another in recognizing and overcoming spiritual attacks?
5. What practical steps can you take daily to armor up spiritually as described in Ephesians 6?

ACTIONABLE STEPS

1. **Cultivate** a deeper prayer life to strengthen your spiritual resilience.
2. **Equip** yourself and your community with knowledge about spiritual warfare and its symptoms.
3. **Engage** in regular spiritual check-ups with a mentor

or accountability partner to maintain spiritual health.

JOURNALING Prompt

Reflect on a time when you experienced spiritual warfare. What were the circumstances? How did you respond? What lessons did you learn about God's protection and your own spiritual readiness?

CHAPTER 10

WALKING IN THE FEAR OF THE LORD

Let's embrace the **fear of the Lord**, for it is the beginning of wisdom and the key to divine protection. This fear isn't about shrinking back; it's about stepping into the fullness of what God has for us with boldness and confidence, knowing that He is always with us, guiding every step we take.

"Let all the earth fear the Lord; Let all the inhabitants of the world stand in awe of Him." - Psalm 33:8 (NKJV)

In our journey together through the teachings of the Bible, we come to a profound concept: the **fear of the Lord**. This isn't about trembling from fright; it's about understanding a deep, reverential awe for God that truly transforms our lives. Here are the essential takeaways and reflections I've gathered for you:

Fearing the Lord isn't about fear in the traditional sense. It's about holding a deep respect and awe that shapes our entire perspective and priorities. This profound reverence helps us see ourselves through God's eyes, rather than just our own. When we embrace the **fear of the Lord**, we learn to define our success not by the applause of others, but by the approval of God. It's seeking His "Well done" that matters most, guiding us to live lives that please Him above all.

Contrary to what you might think, the Bible tells us in Proverbs 14:26 that the **fear of the Lord** actually gives us strong confidence. This type of fear makes us secure in who we are and the divine purpose God has set for our lives. Psalm 2:11 reveals a surprising joy in fearing God. It's about serving the Lord with reverent fear and finding joy in acknowledging that He is in control. This type of fear brings peace and joy because we trust in His sovereign care.

Walking in the **fear of the Lord** isn't just spiritually beneficial; it also protects us from evil. By living in God's ways, we find safety and security from harm, showing us the protective nature of His commandments. The early Church, as described in Acts, flourished significantly by living in the fear of the Lord. This reverence brought them peace and contributed to their rapid growth and strong community.

My own encounter with Jesus was a turning point, making the **fear of the Lord** a reality for me. It was more than just reading or hearing about it; it was a face-to-face meeting that filled me with awe and changed my life forever. As we achieve and succeed, it's crucial to remember that every good thing comes from above. Rather than boasting about our accomplishments, we should point to what God is accomplishing through us, giving Him the glory.

It's easy to either show off or hide our talents. God calls us to use our gifts wisely—**boldly but humbly, always directing the glory back to Him and not to ourselves.** God doesn't just call us to influence; He also shows us how. When we truly **fear the Lord,** He guides our paths and ensures that our work aligns with His purposes, teaching us the right ways to impact our world.

. . .

REFLECTIVE QUESTIONS

1. How does fearing God alter your view of success and influence?
2. Can you recall times when the protective aspect of fearing the Lord was evident in your life?
3. Reflect on an instance when being in God's presence brought you awe and joy. What insights did you gain about God and yourself?
4. How can you ensure that your achievements glorify God rather than yourself?
5. What are some ways that the principle of fearing the Lord can help you overcome insecurities or hesitations about stepping into roles of influence?

ACTIONABLE STEPS

- **Cultivate a Heart of Reverence**: Begin each day by meditating on scriptures that teach about the fear of the Lord. Let these verses guide your thoughts and actions throughout the day, helping you stay aligned with God's wisdom.
- **Equip Yourself with Biblical Truths**: Deepen your understanding of what it means to fear God by joining a Bible study or small group focused on this topic. Share your learnings and listen to others, enriching your journey with diverse perspectives.
- **Engage Others with Humility**: Use your platform, whatever it may be, to highlight how God's grace has

enabled you to achieve your goals. Encourage others by sharing your story, always pointing back to the Lord's work in your life.

57

Journaling **Prompt**

Reflect on the concept that "The fear of the Lord is the beginning of wisdom" (Proverbs 9:10). Journal about a situation where this principle could change your approach or perspective. How might embracing this fear enhance your effectiveness as an influencer in your community or field?

www.ingramcontent.com/pod-product-compliance
Lightning Source LLC
Chambersburg PA
CBHW070919160726
48004CB00003B/1431